This book was written by

I love it when you

You are good at

You inspire me to do many things, especially

I always smile when you

_____

_____

_____

I love doing many things with you especially

_____

_____

_____

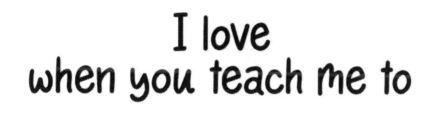

I love
when you teach me to

_____

_____

_____

And
when you tell me not to

My fondest memory of us is when

_____

_____

_____

You cook me delicious meals especially

_____

_____

_____

You are special because

I
admire you because

You always tell the story of the time when

_____

_____

_____

I'm thankful to you because

_____

_____

_____

You make me laugh when

_____

_____

_____

You should be
always

_____

_____

_____

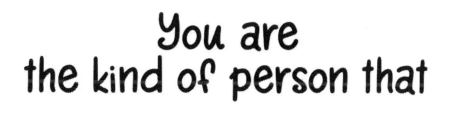

You are
the kind of person that

_____

_____

_____

The most important thing you can do is

_____

_____

_____

My favorite memory with you is

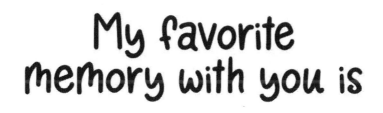

_____

_____

_____

I appreciate
you most when you

_____

_____

_____

I love it when we

The funniest thing you do is

_____

_____

_____

My favorite thing about you is

I remember the time when you and me

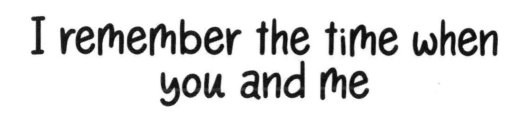

_____

_____

_____

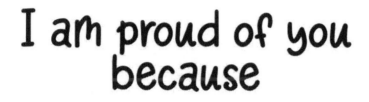

I am proud of you
because

_____

_____

_____

I love you because

The best thing about you is

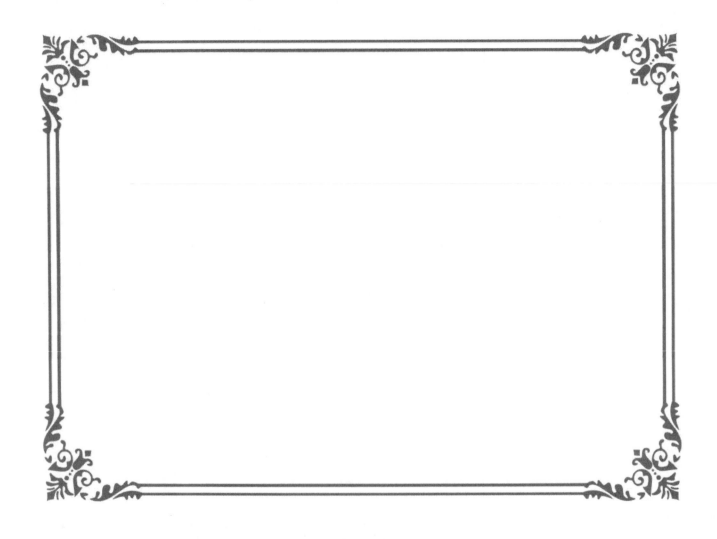

My earliest memory of you is

_____

_____

_____

The most important lesson you ever taught me

_____

_____

_____

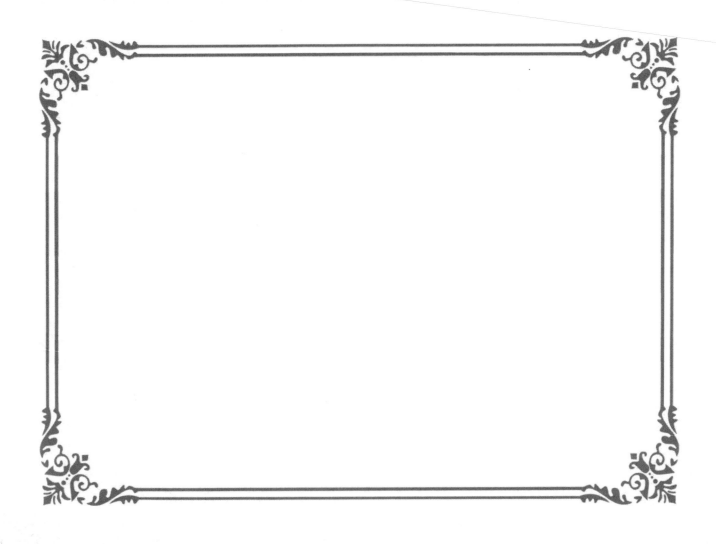

You are my superhero

_____

_____

_____

You are awesome because

_____

_____

_____

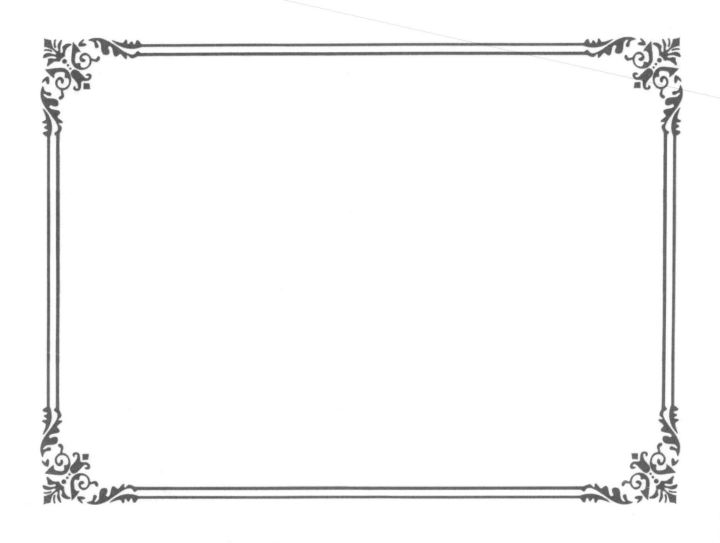

You are my inspiration because

_____

_____

_____

You are my best friend because

_____

_____

_____

You are such a good

You are very
powerful you can do everything

You love it when I

_____

_____

_____

Our favorite thing to do together is

_____

_____

_____

You taught me how to

_____

_____

_____

You are the best

_____

_____

in the world

Thank you
for everything

Printed in Great Britain
by Amazon

17370762R00047